FOOT ON SOIL

ONE BLOOD ALL NATIONS

Published by Krystal Lee Enterprises (KLE Publishing)
Copyright © 2025 by Dr. John L. Curry.

All rights reserved. Please send comments and questions:
KLE Publishing
770-240-0089 Ext. 1
sales@KLEPub.com

To Reach the Author: Dr. John L. Curry

Email: jsconquerors@charter.net

Printed in the United States of America.
All rights reserved. No part of this book may be reproduced or transmitted in any form or by any means, electronic or mechanical, including photocopying, recording, or any information storage and retrieval system without written permission of the publisher except for brief quotations used in reviews, written specifically for inclusion in a newspaper, blog, magazine, or academic paper.

ISBN: 978-1-945066-76-4

Dedication

This book is written for those who have not had the opportunity to place their Foot on Soil on the continent of Africa, whose original name was Alkebulan. The purpose is to bring truth to the world that Africa is not always how the media portrays it. Many people all over the world have been psychologically brainwashed to think that the continent of Africa is a place where uncivilized people live. This book is written to change the narrative about the continent and its people.

Preface

This book is an effort to pass on knowledge to the Black African who lives in the diaspora of how important it is for us to know and understand who we are and where we came from. We are a great people who have built great nations and powerful world civilizations throughout antiquity. We are rediscovering our truth from each other and finding the loopholes in our story. The story of us was once crushed to the earth and shared with us through the lens of oppression. As the truth rises, we rise.

Table of Contents

Chapter 1. Who am I and where did I come from? **7**

Chapter 2. The brainwashing of slaves and historical identity theft. **11**

Chapter 3. The truth about Black African people is rising. **21**

Chapter 4. Foot on Soil in Ghana, West Africa--a mental shift. **25**

Chapter 5. Blacks must detox from slavery. **33**

Chapter 6. Foot on Soil-Athens, Greece **35**

Chapter 7. Foot on Soil-Rome, Italy **39**

Chapter 8. Foot on Soil-Paris, France **47**

Chapter 9. Conclusion **55**

Bibliography **57**

CHAPTER 1

Who Am I, and Where Did I Come From?

Real quick, I was born in Jackson, Mississippi. My father, Samuel Ames, was a sharecropper who signed his name with an "X." My mother, Bertha Vernell Curry, had a third-grade education and was a domestic worker cleaning white people's houses all her life.

I attended Blackburn Elementary School and later Blackburn Middle School. Both schools were all Black. This was before desegregation and the civil rights movement. Old Jim Crow laws were fully implemented. I cannot recall learning any ancient African history while attending elementary or middle school. My knowledge of my ancestry was dark, like my skin.

During school integration in Jackson, Mississippi, from 1970 through 1972, Black students were forcibly transferred to the all-white Wingfield High School. I didn't understand all of the politics of why we had to be forced to learn from people who struggled with our identity. What may have appeared to look like progress at the onset presented a new challenge to being Black. Not just of getting a quality education, but one period. The white students were full of hate, and many white teachers, who professed to be Christians, refused to teach Black students and called us the N-word.

In 1972, I was sent to Waukegan, Illinois, to live with my older sister, and I graduated from Waukegan East High School in 1975. Most of the student body and teachers were white. However, the school had a Black studies class. It was during this time I was told that I looked like the Black African people from Timbuktu. This was said in a very negative way, but

CHAPTER 1

I perceived it to be positive. This was the first time I received a glimpse of "Who am I and where I came from."

Imagine being between a rock and a hard place, and there is where you would have found most of us. The sad part is that most students today still don't get this education. We are called "Black" and stripped of any cultural connections to the continent of Africa. We are called the N-word, and now we use it as a term of endearment for the ignorant to join in if we can't overcome the stigma. To overcome the challenges we face in life, you have to be determined to discover your true identity because it is simply not given to you; you must work for it.

I graduated from Greenville College in 1980. I noticed that no matter what school I went to, there was very little ancient African history taught. Therefore, I began my 40 years of self-study of ancient African history as well as world history. I learned that the American system of education has never been interested in Black liberation. The system of white supremacy was put in place in order to keep the slaves and the descendants of slaves in perceptual blindness so they would never know who they were or where they came from.

Our true history was and still is hidden from us. We should never allow our oppressors to educate us about ourselves. We must educate our own Black people by reading books written by Black historians. Integrating schools and having us learn every level of education from people who do not look like us and many who hate us keeps the ignorant asleep. As long as you learn what keeps you a slave and never change your diet to a balanced consciousness, you will never rise from the ashes. This book intends to change that.

The system of white supremacy will never tell the truth about Black African history because it would diminish white history. We were told that we had no history and that we were uncivilized people who needed to be put into slavery in order to be civilized. We were told we came from a jungle, had no culture, or nothing of value to bring, but needed to be taught or even beat into living a disciplined and worthy life.

They told us we were lazy, ignorant, wore no clothes, and had no formal education. It was Rev. George R. Hawtin of Battlefield, Canada, who

Who Am I, and Where Did I Come From?

wrote in his book called **The Living Creature**, "The Negro, like the man, is perfectly honorable being called in God's word the beast of the field is not of Adam's race. He is very closely related to man." Like Hawtin, many white Christian leaders still believe they are superior to Blacks.

Hawtin continues with his lies, stating, "No Negro civilization has ever arisen. All races of mankind have their civilizations. But history contains no record of a Negro Black civilization." These are all lies; however, many still believe these lies are true.

Isn't it ironic the same people who will tell you there was no successful civilization by Blacks blew the noses off statues in Egypt? They spent years and decades trying to lighten the skin of the Pharaohs in the tombs, but their features tell a different story. Though they try to suppress the truth and whitewash it, the evidence points elsewhere. From sanitation to universities, we can see the residue of Black intelligence. Blacks are treated like fearsome elephants, good for ivory, but not to think using their full member.

Enslaved Africans brought their wisdom, ivory, everywhere they went. Though they were chained like elephants and learned not to run, their divine purpose could never be outbred. The education, beauty, history, and ancestry would shine through no matter what soil they were brought to land on.

In the year of 1619, the first cargo of slaves arrived from the shores of Gore Island in Africa to the 13 colonies of the United States of America. As a direct descendant of slaves, Blacks were the only group of people who did not voluntarily come to America. Our forefathers were kidnapped and sold as they all came by forced migration, which made them prisoners of war.

During the 1600s, 100 years after the middle passage, it is recorded that more than 27 to 30 million Africans died in the ocean. Some were thrown overboard, and some jumped rather than come to America to be slaves.

CHAPTER 1

NOTES:

CHAPTER 2
The Brainwashing of Slaves and Historical Identity Theft.

In the 1700s, slaves were treated worse than animals and were considered the lowest of the beasts of the field. In 1705, slaves were declared real estate. By 1712, the brainwashing of slaves and their identity theft had begun. Willie Lynch, a master-slave trainer whose job was to train slaves to hate themselves and to love their white master, stated, "Take these differences and make them bigger, use fear, distrust, and envy for control purposes. Use age, color or shade, intelligence, size, sex, size of the plantation, status on the plantation, attitude of the owner, whether the slaves live in the valley, on the hill, east, west, north, south, have fine hair, coarse hair, or tall or short. They must love, respect, and trust only us."

This could only happen because the continent of Africa was divided into nations. The white supremacy system, as well as the United States, used these divisions to their advantage. They knew a house divided could not stand. If you could get the Blacks to fight about trible and trivial differences, they would never band together to fight the real threat, enslavement, to obtain freedom.

The brainwashing of slaves and the descendants of slaves is systematic, and the Willie Lynch system of division is still in practice today. In 1778, the United States Constitution approved the 3/5 clause (Article 1, Section 2). It defined the Black slave as property and equal to 3/5 of a man. Despite the assertion of the Declaration of Independence that all men are created equal, the Constitution denied the slave his human rights.

Black people were not included in politics or referenced anywhere that would give them confidence or a sense of identity. It was always in-

CHAPTER 2

tended for the slave to know their place, and that position has been under the feet or leadership of white society. Consider the unjust laws then and look at them now. When will the equality of Blacks be equal to other nations or our white counterparts?

In 1797, psychiatrists came up with a diagnosis for a runaway slave and called it drapetomania. Drapetes was defined as a runaway slave, and mania was defined as mad or crazy. The treatment was whipping the devil out of the slave. It is puzzling to think how any human would come up with such a conclusion. What dog would want to stay with an owner who beat them, worked them from dawn til dusk, sold their children, raped the men and women, and left you feeling worst than the roaches they step on and have your children sweep into the trash?

To see not only the mind but the heart of white people during this time expressed through laws and science should be appalling to humanity. Yet, these same physiological discoveries are being used as foundational text and premises to offer similar findings in social sciences today. Social studies and psychology as a discipline to this day are heavily influenced by white men far more than any other gender or race.

In the 1800s, thousands of Black inventors received patents from the United States of America. A few of these inventions were manufactured carbon, the lubricator for the steam engine, the rotary engine, the letterbox, the railroad signal, the ironing board, the lawn mower, the train alarm, and thousands of other great contributions to this country. Most of these great Black inventors never received payments for their patents. This is historical identity theft.

This is not just a problem that plagues African Americans; this is a vicious cycle that harms the entire continent. A locale rich in soil, people, and priceless artifacts has been pillaged for centuries. America is not the only culprit robbing the continent blind of its people, but the system was created to benefit anyone but Black people.

The white supremacy system says we were and are subhuman while stealing from the continent of Africa. Currently, gold, ivory, diamonds, cotton, rubber, coal, petroleum, cobalt, copper, manganese, iron ore, aluminum, uranium, zinc, and much, much more worth trillions of dollars are

The Brainwashing of Slaves and Historical Identity Theft.

being taken from the continent of Africa. Incredible amounts of African artifacts have been stolen and exported throughout the world.

The Rev. George R. Hawtin, mentioned earlier, used the white supremacy message in the church in order to keep white people from feeling guilty about stealing and killing Black African people. It appears the Rev. Hawtin was not familiar with Genesis 1:27, "So God created man in his own image, in the image of God created he him; male and female created he them." He was also ignorant of the fact that Adam and Eve were not white. The name Adam in Hebrew means reddish brown. According to Newsweek's magazine issue on January 11th, 1988, an article entitled *The Search for Adam and Eve* stated Adam and Eve were both Black and not white.

The continent of Africa must remain poor, and the African people must be viewed as uncivilized in order for the white supremacy system to thrive. Just as the slaves were fed generational lies of having no history, the descendants of slaves were also being fed lies, and today, Black history has been whitewashed, which is historical identity theft.

In my studies of African history, I found men and women such as Imhotep, a multi-genius and a Black Pharaoh of Ancient Egypt in 2200 BC. He was an astronomer, an architect, a physicist, a philosopher, and a poet. He was behind all the great designs in Egypt.

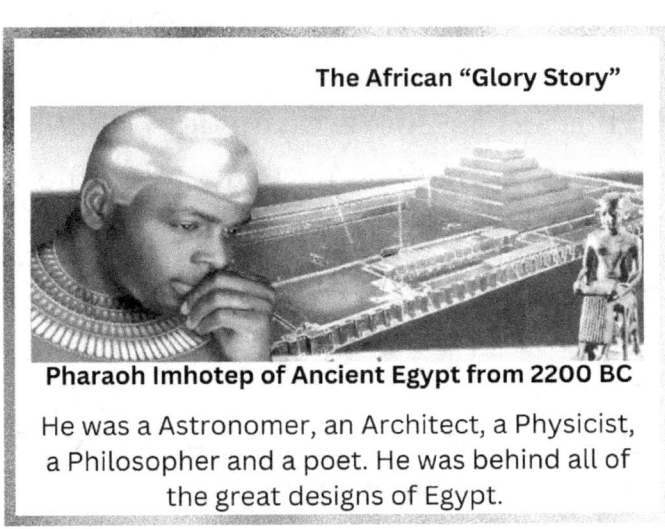

The African "Glory Story"

Pharaoh Imhotep of Ancient Egypt from 2200 BC

He was a Astronomer, an Architect, a Physicist, a Philosopher and a poet. He was behind all of the great designs of Egypt.

Pre-Dynastic Kemet: Nubian Civilization.

- 31 Dynasties
- Dynasties 1-2: King Narmer unifies upper and lower Kemet.
- Dynasties 3-6: Old Kingdom- Pyramid Age. Imhotep.
- Intermediate Period-Upheaval,
- Dynasties 11-12: Middle Kingdom- literary art, literature, religion, the City of Athens, Greece found.
- Dynasties 13-17: Second Intermediate- Asian invasion, widespread destruction.
- Dynasties 18-20: New Kingdom-Temple and Imperial age, King Rameses and Queen Nefertiti, Great Temple Construction and Art.
- Dynasties 21-24: Third Intermediate Period.
- Dynasties 25-26: Late Kingdom Nubian Kings reestablished central government.
- Dynasty 27: Persian invasion, and the capital was moved to Babylon.
- Dynasty 28-29: Capital move to The Western Delta.
- Dynasties 30-31: Last period of rulership of native-born Kemetic Kings.

The Brainwashing of Slaves and Historical Identity Theft.

King Mansa Kankan Musa was a Black ruler from 1312 to 1337. He was worth 400 billion in today's currency. He also helped build the University of Timbuktu during the Mali empire. It was named the University of Sankore.

King Mansa Kankan Musa 1312-1337
He was worth 400 billion in today's currency.

The University of Timbuktu had more than 25,000 students enrolled and 700,000 manuscripts. The core subjects were mathematics, history, astronomy, medicine, law, and others. To complete a degree at the University of Timbuktu, you had to be in attendance for 20 years. This university or school of thought influenced all schools ever created. It was from Black populations that Ivy League schools, the Greeks, and other social or scientific marvels were created.

"The University of Timbuktu"

CHAPTER 2

Some of the greatest minds of Europe came to West Africa in Mali to enroll in the University of Timbuktu—men like Hippocrates, Plato, Aristotle, Socrates, Euripides, and Aristophanes. The University of Timbuktu is the first and the oldest university in the world. Our educational prowess is not the only aspect of Black history we should try to learn from, but also the battles, women, and men who stood up to colonial powers with little support and refused to bow. This boldness and power pumps through your veins, lives in your ancestry, and cries to be remembered.

Remember...

Queen Makeda of Sheba
960 BC

Queen Makeda was an Ethopian who fell in love with King Solomon and gave him many gifts. She was fascinated by his intellect, wisdom, and likely appearance.

Queen Cleopatra of Egypt
69-30 BC

When Queen Cleopatra was 17 years old she almost destroyed Rome and much more.

The African "Glory Story"

King Hannibal IN 247 BC
He had 80,000 Infantry, 12,000 Calvary, 40 African war elephants.

The Brainwashing of Slaves and Historical Identity Theft.

The African "Glory Story"

King Shaka of the Zulus 1818-1828

A strong leader, a military innovator, and a revolutionary warfare man.

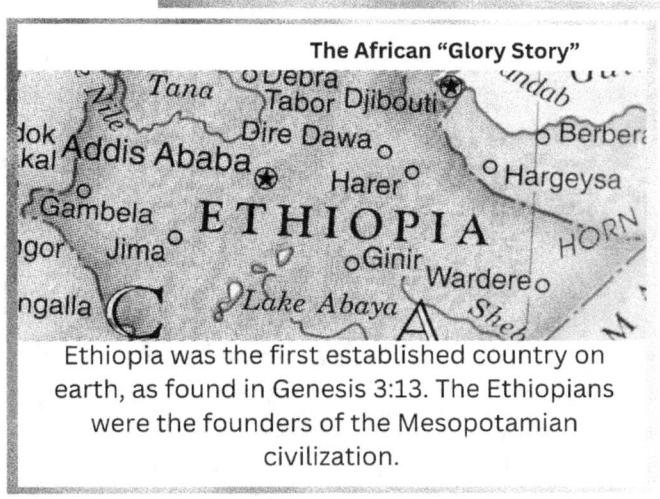

The African "Glory Story"

Ethiopia was the first established country on earth, as found in Genesis 3:13. The Ethiopians were the founders of the Mesopotamian civilization.

The African "Glory Story"

Nimrod, a black man, was the first world ruler and the builder of the tower of Babel.

CHAPTER 2

This ancient Black African history has been whitewashed in an attempt to silence your voice and strangle your hope and progress. Muding the waters of your past with the hopes you would lose interest in where you come from or who you are was the goal. They forgot one fundamental truth: we all long to know who we are; it is the essence of humanity. Downplaying your humanity was a grave misstep, and this is why the conversation and the connection between Black culture can transcend words.

In the Black community, a nod can be an entire conversation. Breathing, eyes, and broken English can be a communication that confounds the wise. So they band your language and scattered your family members, but they underestimated the God you had before you hit the soil of your oppressors. They did not read Genesis 15:13-16 to know the power and intention of your God.

Discrediting you socially, politically, and humanity was to corner your mind. White supremacy hopes to corner you like a weeping dog who feels fear and the doom of nowhere to run. The world claimed that Black African people are uncivilized. But the real question is: "Who civilized who?"

History shows that the first man was Black, and the first woman was also Black, creating the first family. PBS ran a special in the 70s depicting the Black family as the only family with the genes of all nations. Today, the same science is true: there is no nation or race that doesn't carry a DNA strain from a Black culture. Thus, the First Nation and the first builders of ancient world civilization were Black. It was the Black African Kemetic/Egyptian people who had an immense impact on later cultures. It is already said that the Kemetic/Egyptians provided the building blocks for the Greek culture.

Everything the ancient Kemetic/Egyptian people did was a major influence on the Greeks. The Greeks learned how to sculpt limestone from the Africans using materials and techniques in 600 10 B.C. The Kemetic/Egyptian imagery concepts were all over the world. You can find them in architectural forms, on money, and in our day-to-day lives.

The Greeks civilized the Romans; the ancient Greeks had strong cultural influences on the Roman Empire. The Greek influence on Roman

The Brainwashing of Slaves and Historical Identity Theft.

culture is clear in areas such as religion, art, architecture, literature, and philosophy. Many stories and findings already determined were repackaged, labeled with new names, and presented to the people who accepted the cultural norms because they were more of the same.

The Romans enslaved the Greeks. They conquered and influenced France, Spain, and all of Western Europe. Therefore, The Greek, Roman, and European cultures were influenced by Black African/Kemetic Egyptian people, so Who civilized who?

When the truth is told about Black African history, it will always diminish the European story simply because Black people were the first people on the planet. We have had our hands in culture since there was culture. Today, although we have not profited as much as the enslavers, we have influenced every facet of culture. From praise and worship to fashion, education, mechanical inventions, social constructs, style, and attitude were stolen from a Black man or woman.

Power is evident in how we move, think, dress, and respond to conflict. We are resilient, and our strength has been documented in medicine and social constructs. Some slaves underwent procedures with no anesthesia because they said "Blacks were not like white people and did not feel pain." J. Marion Sims performed numerous surgeries on "Black bodies" so he could learn the white counterpart, only to find the strength of one nation wasn't the same for all nations. The original man was built differently, and some would argue that it was perfect (Genesis 1:27).

CHAPTER 2

NOTES:

CHAPTER 3

The Truth About Black African People is Rising.

Dr. Martin Luther King said, "No lie can live forever, and truth crushed to the earth shall rise again."

Dr. John Hendrick Clark said, "History is a clock that people use to tell their political and cultural time of day; it is also a compass people use to find themselves on the map of human geography."

To deny a people their history is to deny they ever existed. There have been movements to whitewash and erase Black African history for over 500 years. As Black people, we have never relied on the white supremacy system to educate Black people about our history.

The world has no history without Black African history because our history came from Africa. Black people civilized the world. Black history started in the Holy Bible and in the book of Genesis with Adam and Eve. To deny Black African history is to deny the truth of the Holy Bible. All of this happened long before the transatlantic slave trade in America.

The white supremacy system does not want slave history, Jim Crow, the Civil Rights Movement, and structural racism to be talked about or taught in schools. Over 30 state legislatures across the country have introduced a bill to limit the discussion of racial history. The infection of racism is still a major infection in our nation. Overlooking the elephant sure won't make it disappear.

Over 300 books predominantly written by Black authors discussing race have been banned in the last year alone. Books may be banned, but

CHAPTER 3

history cannot be erased. The social media landscape is dominating the world. Facebook, YouTube, WhatsApp, Instagram, TikTok, WeChat, Snapchat, Ozone, Spotify, X (Twitter), and many other social media websites are just a few of the platforms that can be used to teach history all over the world. History can never be discarded.

The question is, if America's history is so great, why is she trying to hide it from her children and the world? The white supremacy system loves to play three roles: first role of the victim, which says Blacks and all other groups are trying to take America from us. The second role is the victor, which says we must take our country back in order to make America great again, and the third role is no responsibility, no accountability to any other race group but the white supremacy system. This reminds me of the scripture John 10:10, "The thief cometh not, but for to steal, and to kill, and to destroy: I am come that they might have life, and that they might have it more abundantly."

The world is in a genetic war for survival for all white people. The white birth rate is below 1.8, which cannot sustain any population. White birth rates are declining all over the world. Black and brown people have the dominant gene of melanin, while whites have the regressive gene.

When the white race mixes with the Black and brown race, the Black and brown race dominates and determines the race. This is why whites will never fully integrate with Black and brown people because it would cause the extinction of the white race. It is not about the border but about white survival in order to create a white utopia in America.

Long before the white supremacy system created race, the Bible records in the book of Genesis 10:1-32 the 70 nations. In Genesis 10:1-5, the Sons of Japheth represented the 14 Caucasoid nations, who are known today as the white European people. Genesis 10:6-20, the Sons of Ham represented the 30 Negroid nations which are the Black people, and Genesis 10:21-29 the Sons of Shem represented the 26 Mongoloid nations which are the Asian people.

There was no such thing as race or racism until the white supremacy system decided to pull all the European nations together to rule the world based on skin color. In 1452 and 1455, Pope Nicholas V formally supported Spain and Portugal's mass kidnapping and enslavement of Africans because he said it would help to Christianize the enslaved people. Also, Pope Innocent had 14 slaves who worked for the Vatican. The Pope said if you are going to enslave any people, enslave Blacks because they are hard workers.

At this point, the white supremacy system used their whiteness to try and dominate the world. They depicted Jesus as white. They did not stop there. They went to heaven and depicted God, all the angels, and all the heavenly hosts as white, idolizing whiteness to godliness. This is an abomination and a violation of the second commandment. Exodus 20:4 says, "Thou shall not make unto thee any graven image, or any likeness of anything that is in heaven above, or that is in the earth beneath, or that is in the water under the earth."

In 1869, Francis Galton and Ernst Rudin introduced the concept of the Science of Eugenics. In Greek, Eugenics means "good in stock." In 1870, psychologist Herbert Spencer took Galton's term further by coining the term "Survival of the Fittest." In 1887, G. Stanley Hall, founder of the American Journal of Psychology, stated that Africans, Indians, and Chinese were members of an adolescent race in a stage of incomplete growth.

This is the beginning of colorism, which has moved into the caste system, which says the lighter the skin tone, the greater the privilege. We are where we are because the white supremacy system has brought us here. The division and colorism within the Black Community are a product of slavery. In 2025, those with darker complexions can feel inferior to those who are not. For pageantry and other programs, European hair is needed to be beautiful or desired.

These psychosocial false prophets are still operating in the science of Eugenics, hoping for an all-white America. Using modern-day technology to zero in on "Black genes" will not transition the plan God has for the Black community. The gift and blessing of the people of God will not be erased. They're trying to start a racial holy war (Ra Ho Rah) in America, which is ironic.

Race has nothing to do with a holy war. The real war is spiritual, and the evil spirits behind eugenics and cruel science are mere puppets of evil spirits who hate humanity. Fallen angels don't hate just white or Black people; they hate all humankind. Divide and conquer is the plan of the evil spirits that collide and manipulate the fears of men and women to bring destruction and disunity.

If this war is heightened and a full battle is fought between white and Black people, this nation will have a problem like all other nations attempting to remove the Seed of Abraham. All Americans will lose, and it will be the downfall of this nation. What nation could stand in the presence of an angry God and not be humbled?

The Truth About Black African People is Rising.

NOTES:

CHAPTER 3

CHAPTER 4

Foot on Soil in Ghana, West Africa--A Mental Shift.

Growing up in Jackson, MS, my mother raised eight children alone. On many occasions, I would go with her to clean white people's houses. She was a hard worker and taught me the value of work. I would watch her and the other maids, with their white dresses and Black coats, waiting for the bus; some were given a ride by the owners of the homes, and others would ride the bus or walk.

As a young Black boy, I could not wait to get home to watch the Legend of Tarzan, seeing a white man swinging from tree to tree on a vine. He was called the ing of the jungle as he ruled the jungle. This was and still is the white supremacy system using propaganda to influence and brainwash Blacks in America and Africa to think that the white man is the only one who can save the Black African from himself.

Even as a young Black boy, while watching the Legend of Tarzan, I was always rooting for the Black Jujus, who were the Black natives in the jungle. I would ask myself, is this who I am? And where is this jungle?

Because of my dark skin, I was called names such as spook, Blackie, and many other hurtful names. I was told many times by some of my elders that when I did something wrong, they were going to knock me back to Timbuktu. I would ask them where Timbuktu is. Some would say in Africa. I would ask them where is Africa? And they would stop talking as though they did not know where it was.

As I have shared with you in previous chapters, as a people we have a great history, and we are a great people. One of my major goals in

CHAPTER 4

Foot on Soil in Ghana, West Africa--A Mental Shift.

life was to make it to the continent of Africa. As a historian, I have studied and done research on Black African history for over 40 years. I have also learned from other Black historians such as Chancellor Williams, Dr. John Henrik Clarke, Amos N. Wilson, Dr. Ivan Van Sertima, Yosef Ben Johannan, Cheikh Anta Diop, Dr. Francis Gress Welsing, Shahrazad Ali, Dr. Claud Anderson and many others.

Many of these Black historians have visited the continent of Africa. My life goal to visit the continent of Africa finally came to fruition in October 2022. My wife and I put **"Foot on Soil"** in Ghana, West Africa.

We were very excited to depart from St. Louis, MO, arriving in Washington, DC to prepare for a 10-hour flight to Accra, Ghana, West Africa. We kept telling each other that we were going to the continent of Africa. We arrived at 2:00 p.m. in Accra, the capital of Ghana, West Africa. When we departed from the airport, I kneeled down and kissed the soil, and when I stood up, all we saw were Black people.

As our tour guide drove us to our hotel in Accra, we saw many Black Africans who looked like family members in America. We went sightseeing through the city and saw the administrative area punctuated with elegant villas built during the first half of the 19th Century.

We explored the old quarters of Jamestown, inhabited by the local population known as the Ga. On the ocean shore of the Mediterranean Sea, we saw the native people's life fully unfold. We saw the creative genius of the Ghanaian people who specialized in the building of fantasy coffins. These special handcrafted coffins reflected many shapes, fruits, animals, fish, cars, and airplanes, the only limit is in the imagination. These flamboyant coffin designs are collected worldwide and exhibited in museums.

We visited the Kumasi region, the historical and spiritual capital of the old Ashanti Kingdom. This is a city proud of its past and shown through the people even in the present. It has a flourishing economy thanks to the exploitation of its gold mines and its forest, of which many trees provide medicine for the world. The Ashanti people were one of the most powerful nations in Africa until the end of the 19th Century when the British annexed Ashanti country to their Gold Coast colony. The Ashanti are a great people and treated us like the family that we knew from

CHAPTER 4

Foot on Soil in Ghana, West Africa--A Mental Shift.

a long time ago.

With nearly 1,000,000 inhabitants, Kumasi is a great city with one of the biggest markets in Africa. One of the amazing things about the Ashanti people is their ability to produce every type of Ashanti craft, such as leather goods, pottery, beautiful Kente cloth designs, and much more. The Ashanti people in Ghana and the Ivory Coast are by far the two largest producers of cocoa, accounting for more than 50% of the world's cocoa. My wife and I observed the process of making chocolate from cocoa. We were also dressed in Kente clothes as Kings and Queens.

We went on a safari in Kumasi Mole National Park, known as West Africa's biggest game park. It is the biggest elephant sanctuary in Africa, having more than 600 elephants, antelopes, an unnumbered amount of primates, and other game.

CHAPTER 4

32

Foot on Soil in Ghana, West Africa--A Mental Shift.

Next, we visited the ancient Islamic of Larabanga. This is a memorable Sudanese architecturally designed and historic mosque that was built by the Moorish traders. Seeing this structural design reminded me of the ventilation system I read about that the University of Timbuktu-Sankore had during the Mali empire, which was also built by the Moorish traders.

We visited the Elmina and Cape Coast slave castles, which were built by the Swedes from 1657 to 1664. It changed hands many times and was conquered by the Danes, the Dutch, and the Fanti, a local tribe. The castles served as a trading post for the European nations and as the headquarters of British colonial administrations for the Gold Coast colony.

CHAPTER 4

While touring the castles, my wife and I were hit with almost uncontrollable emotions, seeing the place where slaves, our ancestors, took their last bath and were transferred to the medieval castle dungeons, which were dark, damp, and dirty. While walking through the dungeons we could almost feel the pain of our ancestors and saw the centuries of blood stains and waste on the concrete floor.

I was so moved that I asked for and was given permission to give a speech at the Cape Coast Castle entitled "The Message to the Black Diamond: Unite or Die." Being able to place **Foot on Soil** meant everything to us. Being on the continent of our origin was the liberation of our minds.

NOTES:

CHAPTER 4

CHAPTER 5

Blacks Must Detox From Slavery.

Black Africans were brought to America in 1619. We worked as actual slaves for 244 years. There were 100 years of Jim Crow, separate but so-called equal. This was a standard established by the Supreme Court, Plessy versus Ferguson, in 1896, which undergirded racial segregation.

Those who enslaved Blacks in America and around the world instituted the most heinous and vicious violent acts towards the Black Slaves. The enslaved people went through contextual violence, that is, strategic violence, territorial violence, and ritualistic violence, and they went through horrification, brutalization with traumatic factors, and abandonment.

The trauma from slavery was passed down through the enslaved people's genes. In epigenetics, Dr. Rachel Yehuda, a professor of psychiatry at Icahn School of Medicine at Mount Sinai, conducted in-depth research into the intergenerational general transmission of trauma (Slave Trauma). The Black African enslaved experienced the transgenerational transmission of slave pathology. Sociologist Dr. Joy DeGrug studied post-traumatic slave syndrome and Stockholm syndrome. Stockholm syndrome is when victims love their captors more than themselves.

Detoxing and decolonizing the Black African's mind is a meaningful and active discipline practice to heal from the forces of slavery and colonialism that penetrate the subjugation and exploitation of the Black African's mind, body, spirit, and land. The Black African must detoxify and declutter his mind from the odious toxicity of white supremacy and brainwashing because of the master-slave trainer Willie Lynch. As a people, there has to be a conscious decision to rewrite truth where there have been

CHAPTER 5

lies.

Multi-generational oppression from centuries of chattel slavery and institutional racism can leave a chemical mark on a person's genes whose forefathers were in fact enslaved. The intergenerational transmission, epigenetic mechanisms such as colonialism and slavery, and displacement of trauma can affect the next generation.

Shackles remain from the physical and mental violence the enslaved were subjected to. The Black Africans must go through a detoxification process of what has been beaten into them. The Black Africans are not animals nor property to be used and discarded. For the last 400 years, Blacks have been responding to white supremacy, stating, "Get your foot off my neck; we are men, women, and children, and our forefathers are builders and founders of great ancient world civilization." It is only when we truly know where we came from that we will truly know where we are going.

When we know who our forefathers were, as discussed earlier, and we know men such as Dr. Thomas O. Mensah, a Black man who is the inventor of fiber optics and nanotechnology. Who also built the first bullet train, is responsible for the Internet, and creating a Black Disney World. He is an urban intellectual who holds 14 patents and is the founder of the National Academy of Inventors.

Dr. Mark Dean, a Black man, invented the computer processor chip, holds three of nine patents, and is the co-creator of the IBM personal computer released in 1981. Dr. Emeagwali Phillip of Nigeria invented the Internet and cell phones with the help of Mr. Henry T. Samson and Jesse Lee Russell.

When we study who we were, we will know who we are, and when we know who we are, our minds will be detoxified. We will move in the Black African pride of loving ourselves and being unified.

Blacks Must Detox From Slavery.

NOTES:

CHAPTER 5

CHAPTER 6

Foot on Soil-Athens, Greece

After studying ancient African culture and having visited the continent of Africa with- **Foot on Soil**, I can clearly see the influence that Egyptian culture has had on Europe in areas such as religion, art, architecture, literature, and philosophy. My focus with this book, **Foot on Soil**, will be to show how the ancient Egyptian culture had a strong cultural influence on Greece and how Ancient Greek culture had a strong cultural influence on the Roman Empire and the Roman Empire, after taking Greeks as slaves conquered and influenced France, Spain and all of western Europe. Therefore, they all developed their civilization based on Africa.

The Egyptian civilization lasted more than 3,000 years, and the Greek philosophers, such as Hippocrates, Plato, Aristotle, Socrates, Euripides, and Aristophanes, learned from over 25,000 professors at the University of Timbuktu-Sankore in the Mali Empire. The focus of the study was astronomy, mathematics, history, medicine, and more.

Plato studied in Egypt for 13 years and told his students to go to Egypt if they wanted to study the minds of great philosophers. Pythagoras studied philosophy, geometry, and medicine in Egypt for 22 years. Thales was the first Greek philosopher to study in Egypt for seven years. Hypocrites, who was called the Father of Medicine, recognized the Egyptian multi-genius Imhotep as the Father of Medicine. The "Pythagorean Theorem" was used to build the pyramids in Egypt 1,000 years before Pythagorean was born. Herodotus, a Greek historian, described ancient Egypt as the Cradle of Civilization.

Some of the Greek customs include over 4,000 traditional dances

CHAPTER 6

Foot on Soil-Athens, Greece

and the celebration of "Name Day" of the Saints that bears the name rather than their own birthday. As I walked the streets of Athens –**Foot on Soil**, visited the Acropolis, the Acropolis Museum, and went to the beautiful city of Delphi, where I could see the Egyptian influence. The Temple of Apollo at Delphi was the first temple located in Delphi, serving as a sanctuary for the god of Apollo. Delphi, Greece, a city of the ancient world, was amazing. The houses were built on the slopes of the mountains.

Greece is officially a secular state. However, 97% of Greeks are Orthodox-Roman and Greek Catholics, but in Athens, it is slightly lower because of the many immigrants and foreigners of different faiths. The infiltration of immigrants is causing serious issues within Greece. It is viewed as a potential threat to population growth.

The worldwide white birth rate is 1.8 children, while 2.1 is the necessary number to sustain a population. Therefore, the issue concerning Black and brown people or immigration and migrating to Greece is the issue of the white low birth rate. Therefore, whites are afraid of genetic annihilation, and this is why Greece is moving away from scholarly conversations and open dialogue to the adaptation of white supremacy, which is outside of her character, seeing all Black and brown people as a threat to their genetic survival. Blacks in Greece were called Black Greecian in ancient times, and the shift from seeing Black people as teachers to slaves, from a people similar to them to an object less than a dog, was European influence.

Visiting Athens, Greece, in October was the perfect time. The weather was great. Bring your camera or phone to take great pictures of the incredible skyline views of the city and the many spectacular ruins. Also, make sure you wear trainers with a solid grip. The Acropolis is full of slippery marble on the ground. Getting around the city was easy, restaurants were plentiful, and the food was delicious.

Nothing is better than **Foot on Soil**. When you put your foot where your ancestors roamed, where your history lies, and investigate yourself, it strengthens your bond to who you are. What you value, you will invest in. Where your heart is, there will be your treasure also (Matthew 6:21).

CHAPTER 6

NOTES:

CHAPTER 6

CHAPTER 7

Foot on Soil-Rome, Italy

Rome, Italy's major religion is Roman Catholic. Emperor Constantine was said to be the one who first legalized Christianity in the 1st Century, 313 CE. The culture is built on art, architecture, and fashion. There are 280 fountains, fifty of which are monumental. Some of the major traditions are the Festival of the Grapes, Carnival, Corpus Domino, and Rome's birthday.

While in Rome–**Foot on Soil**, our driver shared with us some of Rome's history. He said Rome is an old city with many old buildings, just like France. Speaking with someone who actually lives in the city and experiences the culture was rewarding. Most of the drivers we had were very friendly and open to talking about the city and culture, while others did not speak English or simply did not want to talk.

The first place that we visited in the city of Rome, Italy, was the Colosseum, which was within walking distance from our hotel. **Foot on Soil**, we could feel the stories that were not told and visualize the many through seeing the ruins and lasting structures of what was many years ago. The Colosseum is an Amphitheatre built in Rome under the Flavian emperors of the Roman Empire. It is also called the Flavian Amphitheatre. It is an elliptical structure made of stone, concrete, and tuff and stands four stories tall at its highest point. It only took 8 years to build the Colosseum, which was built by mostly Black Jewish slaves and overseen by Roman engineers and craftsmen.

The tour guide said that the lions were eating Christians, but many of these Christians were criminals; some were posing as Christians. It is

CHAPTER 7

Foot on Soil-Rome, Italy

estimated that roughly 500,000 lives were taken from the days of both the gladiator battles and human sacrifice. It was rather eerie to stand in a place created to glorify the horror of human sacrifice for entertainment, but we have to put our **Foot on Soil**.

After our visit to the Colosseum, we went to visit the Vatican, Sistine Chapel, and Saint Peter's Basilica–**Foot on Soil**. The tour was very long and interesting. Seeing St. Peter's Basilica added about a mile of additional walking to the tour. We saw many paintings and sculptures created by Michelangelo. The people were blatantly naked everywhere we went, including the paintings of White Jesus. I could not understand why most of Michelangelo's paintings and sculptures were people who were naked to the point of perversion.

It was said that nudity was used to show off a perfect male body suitable for athletic activity in the art of war; moreover, it was a sign of both external and internal perfection. The artwork covered the walls and the ceilings. Nudity was pervasive. I found the paintings were disgraceful in what was supposed to be a sacred place. The pope had to approve the artwork before it was painted.

It was said that there was a war, and many bodies were buried under the ground of the space in which worship takes place at the Vatican. This brought up many questions: why would the church worship on the grounds where bodies are buried? It was said that the Pope wanted to build a new church, so he covered up the bodies to build a new church. Vatican City is built on a burial ground, but I thought where the Church of God sat must be "holy ground" (Exodus 3:5). Moses had to remove his shoes, and King David couldn't build the temple because there was murder on his hands (2 Samuel 7:4-17 and 1 Chronicles 22).

Biblical scholars have called the Catholic Church "The Great Harlot" or the "Whore of Babylon" of Revelation 17 and 18. She has been poisoning the world for over 3,000 years with the Doctrine of Discovery, the opiate for the masses, in which a white Jesus is presented as the opiate for the masses. This plan has a sinister objective: to get the world to believe in a white Jesus as the Messiah to undergird the doctrine of white supremacy. The Catholic Church is still reaching for serious political power as well as spiritual power. The church's history is filled with blood, betrayal, pedo-

CHAPTER 7

philia, rape, and money grabs to dominate the world. Elected seats were purchased, and getting into heaven was reduced to how much you could spend before and after you died to buy your way out of purgatory or that of your loved ones. This doctrine did not get done away with until recently in history. The concepts identify more with Roman paganism than biblical sound doctrine.

The Roman emperor Constantine legalized Christianity and promoted religious tolerance in 313 CE through the edict of Milan. He also legalized and established Christmas Day to be celebrated on the 25th of December, 326 CE. The issue with laws being passed that appear to be holy and are not is that people can follow the decoy and miss its true meaning. Christ did not come to preach a religion; he came to preach the Kingdom of God and lead a holy reformation. Where the people are not hypocrites like the Jews in the Sanhedrin but restore divine order, love, and grace for all people.

God is not a respecter of person (Acts 10:34), yet He knows the hearts of men (Luke 16:15) and knows His children (Galatians 3:26.-28). The facts are Jesus Christ the Messiah never started a religion or preached Christianity. Jesus Christ only preached the Kingdom of God. He proved that the Kingdom included women and men, Greeks, Jews, and Gentiles.

CHAPTER 7

Foot on Soil-Rome, Italy

All who believe can be welcomed into the Kingdom of God and become Children of God. Race and religion are not God's factors but human grievances.

After placing "**Foot on Soil**" and seeing the grandeur of The Vatican, there are many contradicting facts against the overblown feeling of self-importance of the Catholic church. In Rome, like elsewhere, the white birth rate is 1.2 children, while 2.1 is the necessary number to sustain the population. The issue concerning Black and brown people and immigration to Rome is the issue of the low white birth rate. Therefore, whites are afraid of genetic annihilation. Africans and South Asia people are the largest number of immigrants to Rome to find jobs and a safe place to live.

Overall, October in Rome, Italy, was wonderful. Transportation is readily available, and there are lots of good places for fine dining. I am glad I had the opportunity to place my **Foot on Soil**. To walk where Christ did, to experience the wind, to see the sites, and to feel the history was euphoric and impactful.

CHAPTER 7

NOTES:

CHAPTER 8

Foot on Soil-Paris, France

Paris, France, identifies as 66% Catholic, 9% Muslim, and the rest Jewish, Buddhist and other. Paris is famous for its dedication to the arts. The French state has a strong record of supporting the arts, literature, music, visual arts, and otherwise. It has a tradition of eating long lunches, gathering with family, and embracing unity.

On our first day in Paris, there was pouring down rain. It took 2 1/2 hours to get from the airport to our hotel. It rained at least once a day, every day that we were in Paris–**Foot on Soil**. On the way to the hotel, our driver told us how dangerous the city of Saint-Denis was as we passed through it. He said at night, the city gets loud, and lots of drugs and partying happen all night. He went on to say the dilapidated architecture of the city has a great design, but the buildings are very old and are in stages of decay.

He also gave us his opinion of President Emmanuel Macron. He said the president has a bad relationship with the continent of Africa and many nations in Africa. I did not find the citizens of Paris to be friendly personally. Racial divide can be felt the moment you arrive and throughout your stay. Their opinions of Blacks are not hidden but alive in plain sight today, in their politics, and throughout their history with Black nations.

Many Blacks, except the Americans, are not entreating. Several appeared to be of African descent. Ambassador Ankana Chihombori Quao stated France would be a third-world country without the continent of Africa. The money that is extorted or controlled by France through modern-day slavery is appalling. Forcibly banking with France, buying your

CHAPTER 8

money, paying fees to hold or store your money, and then paying again to trade your money sounds like stealing on an entirely different level. Where would the EURO be without the Black populations propping up their dollar yet these nations they volunteered to test COVID vaccinations on before approval? They still see the Black nations as their guinea pigs.

Our first tour was of the Eiffel Tower. It was stunning. The structural engineer was Gustave Eiffel, who died on December 27th, 1923. During the construction of the Eiffel Tower, it surpassed the Washington Monument to become the tallest human-made structure in the world, a title it held for 41 years until the Chrysler building in New York City was finished in 1930. While at the summit, we could see the whole city of Paris, which was magnificent. I found the city structures to be very similar to the designs in Rome. Everything was easily accessible, with lots of restaurants and Ubers available whenever needed.

The Palace of Versailles had over 90,000 works of art, The Hall of Mirrors, the King's and Queen's Grand Apartments, the Museum of the History of France, and so much more. The Seine River Cruise was relaxing, which my wife and I took. The negative I saw was that the water was brown, and I could not imagine the Olympic teams swimming in it.

We visited the Museum Quai Branly. It is a museum designed by French architect Jean Nouvel to feature the Indigenous art and cultures of Africa, Asia, Oceania, and the Americas. History tells us that 90 to 95% of those who built France were African, and the other 5% were Europeans who came from Poland, Britain, and Greece. One of our drivers told us that Paris, France, was built by African slaves after the city was burned. The Africans and Arabs built the city back up, and now the government wants all the African immigrants to leave France.

The immigration factor is continuing, man's inhumanity to man, if you're not European in France, you will stand the chance of being mistreated and viewed as a potential threat. The dominance and ability to achieve vision is intimidating. The heart of Pharoah was the same: to fear the people they used and abused, bonding with nations who sought vengeance or war with them. Apparently, the struggle of being Black, not being wanted but needed, not being appreciated but tolerated is all over the world.

The worldwide white birth rate is 1.8 children, while 2.1 is the nec-

Foot on Soil-Paris, France

CHAPTER 8

essary number to sustain the population. If you haven't seen the problem, I question if we are seeing the writing on the wall. The actions of nations to use white supremacy to rule the world are wrong. The Bible says in Proverbs 22:23, "For the Lord will plead their cause, and spoil the soul of those that spoiled them." Stealing comes with a curse, seeing robbery and injustice and turning a blind eye also has a consequence. Proverbs 29:24 repeats, "Whoso is partner with a thief hateth his own soul: he heareth cursing, and bewrayeth it not."

Therefore, the issue concerning Black and brown people and immigration and migrating to France is the issue all the same: white low birth rates. The fear and anxiety of these nations and those who uplift the genocide of Black and brown nations are the same; they are afraid of their own genetic annihilation. This is why France sees Black and brown people as a threat to their genetic survival. White Europeans must come to understand they cannot claim to be supreme when they're carrying the melanin recessive genes.

To think of how white people can be outbred or genetically aborted by nature is scary. Being born with small amounts of melanin is a health risk that is coming more and more to the forefront. It is rumored among scientists that white people can go extinct in the next 30 to 50 years. The white supremacy doctrine is hemorrhaging over the globe and causing fallout and fear.

White supremacy is not only causing political fallout, it is also plaguing the church. The division between white evangelicals and the Black church will not be able to last any longer. In years past, the white church could survive with religion, but in years to come, you will need to be a clear follower of the Word of God .

Heaven will not be segregated, and there will be no special seats for white people separated from Black people. History would tell us if that were the case, they would be put away from Christ. He is drawn in older text with brown skin, wooly hair, and he was believed to look more like a Black person than a European, as pictured in older paintings. The lies have to fall down. The images must be burned; the hypocrisy and blasphemy must end.

White supremacy runs contrary to the Kingdom of God. And this is why whites or white evangelicals who identify with the white supremacy doctrine cannot escape this judgment. They will never be Kingdom Citizens when they refuse to embrace the body of Christ, including people of all colors and cultures. For whites to follow Matthew 5:44, "But I say to you, Love your enemies and pray for those who persecute you;" Whites and white evangelicals must humble themselves to the Word of God.

To whites, loving all as themselves means they must decrease so that God can increase. John had to decrease so that Christ could increase. Our agendas must fade so that Christ's influence can increase. This could be seen as self-annihilation if you are trying to preserve the white supremacy doctrine that "white people" are superior to others. Following this chapter and verse rules out being your own god. Those who practice white supremacy have removed Christ as their Lord and Savior and erected themselves as god and above all.

For whites to follow Matthew 6:33, "But seek ye first the kingdom of God, and his righteousness; and all these things shall be added unto you." To whites, uplifting white supremacy would mean self-affiliation. You cannot seek the Kingdom of God when trying to build your own kingdom on earth like how they see themselves as trying to be God. This is devilish and reminds me of Isaiah 14:12-15.

12 How art thou fallen from heaven, O Lucifer, son of the morning! how art thou cut down to the ground, which didst weaken the nations!

13 For thou hast said in thine heart, I will ascend into heaven, I will exalt my throne above the stars of God: I will sit also upon the mount of the congregation, in the sides of the north:

14 I will ascend above the heights of the clouds; I will be like the most High.

15 Yet thou shalt be brought down to hell, to the sides of the pit.

Those who believe in white supremacy doctrine are being beguiled to believe their witness makes them like God and not their heart, actions, and love. This is a lie born from the father of lies, satan, the great deceiver. This doctrine has been judged, and those who follow it will end up in the

CHAPTER 8

pit, the lowest depths of hell.

For whites to follow Matthew 22:39, which reads, "And the second should be like unto it, though shall love thy neighbor as thy self." To whites and this supporting white supremacy, that would mean self-annihilation. To love everybody would mean possibly marrying other groups, and these groups, if they are Black or brown, have a genetically more dominant gene that would overshadow the recessive trait of "white."

For whites to follow Ephesians 4:6, "One God and Father of all, who is above all, and through all, and in you all." To whites would mean self-annihilation because they believe they are the one body and supreme race. White pastors have learned how to act based on 2 Timothy 3:5, which reads, Having a form of godliness, but denying the power thereof: from such turn away."

How can you say you are a child of love, when God is Love and turn away the brothers and sisters you see because of their skin color? 1 John 4:8 reads, "He that loveth not knoweth not God; for God is love." In 1 John 4:20 the bible reads, " If a man say, I love God, and hateth his brother, he is a liar: for he that loveth not his brother whom he hath seen, how can he love God whom he hath not seen?" It is impossible to please God with thoughts of men. God's ways are higher than man's ways, and he is the only just God and wise ruler (Isaiah 55:8-9).

I wonder if most whites subconsciously are angry with God because they have the recessive gene, and their response is to afflict humanity to hurt God. It reminded me of the Tower of Babel when man thought of warring with God, and he cursed parts of humanity to be like monkey and ape people (Gen. 11:1-9, Jasher Chapter 9:22-39). The Father judged those who thought to war with him and sent 70 angels to deal with 600,000 humans working to build the tower.

The Tower of Babel proves that men can accomplish great things by working in unison, but it also proves no one can hold back the hand of God to judge. When He judged, he confounded languages, cut off people from the earth, and scattered people. The same God who did it before can and should expect no less for Him to do it again. He says in Malachi 3:6, "For I am the Lord, I change not; therefore ye sons of Jacob are not con-

Foot on Soil-Paris, France

sumed."

The same God you were compelled to believe in when you were in need extends truth on this day. Don't throw away the Hand of God and choose to take out your anger on the world of Black people like in the past 400 years. White people and white evangelicals, you cannot save yourselves. Those who try to save themselves will lose themselves, but those who lose themselves for Christ's sake will find themselves (Matthew 16:25).

The work humanity is trying to do has already been done. There is a Savior, a way–the right way. God has already made way for your escape through His Son, Jesus the Christ. Repent, repent, repent; and accept Him as your Savior before it is too late.

CHAPTER 8

NOTES:

CONCLUSION

In my travels to Europe, I have noticed most European countries are white-male nations. Whiteness is an oppositional construct, meaning racism by intent. It will oppose any person, group, or nation who threatens the white supremacy lifestyle.

The issues concerning migration and immigration are issues concerning the dominant melanin genes. White Europeans have recessive melanin genes, and Black and brown people have the dominant melanin genes. When the Black and brown people mix with the white Europeans, they believe it will cause a genetic annihilation of the white race.

I leave this book with verses to ponder and summarize the internal dialogue of my travels by putting my **Foot on Soil** in nations that perpetuated human violence around the world. Although I see the vile nature and the evidence of corruption, I also see the miracle and promise of God fulfilled. He will bless his children no matter where they live; he has been faithful throughout their ages and incredible circumstances.

The thief cometh not, but for to steal, and to kill, and to destroy: I am come that they might have life and that they might have it more abundantly (John 10:10). And hath made of one blood all nations of men for to dwell on all the face of the earth, and have determined the times before appointed, and the bounds of their habitation (Acts 17:26).

We love him because he first loved us. If a man says, I love God, and hateth his brother; he is a liar: for he that loveth not his brother whom he hath seen, how can he love God whom he hath not seen? And this com-

CHAPTER 9

mandment has we from him, that he who loveth God love his brother also (1 John 4:19-21). Seek ye first the Kingdom of God, and his righteousness; And all these things shall be added unto you (Matthew 6:33). Whatever you need for life, make God your source.

And I close by saying...work out your own salvation with fear and trembling. Philippians 2:12 reads, "Wherefore, my beloved, as ye have always obeyed, not as in my presence only, but now much more in my absence, work out your own salvation with fear and trembling." Know this, you will not go to hell or heaven as a group, but you will go as a individual. Therefore, you must take accountability and responsibility for your own salvation.

Know what you believe, know how and why you believe and remember tomorrow is not promised while keeping it kingdom. Breathe daily, that is to inhale the Word of God as you read the Word of God, and exhale the Word of God as you pray. As you breathe in the natural, you must also breathe in the spiritual. Do this daily and you are building a relationship with God and that is "Keeping it Kingdom."

"The World Already Knows Who We Are--We are the Most Brilliant, The Most Excellent, The Most Creative, The Most Resilient People on the Face of the Earth and We Must Show One Love to Ourselves. One Blood. All Nations."

Conclusion

NOTES:

CHAPTER 9

BIBLIOGRAPHY

1. The Holy Bible, King James Version

2. Wood, Forrest G., The Arrogance of Faith, 1860

3. Hawtin, George R., The Living Creature, 1974

4. Galton, Francis, The Eugenic Theory, 1869

5. J. H. Clarke/ V. Harding, Slave Trade & Slaver, 1970

6. Hebrew Greek Key Study Bible

7. Creating Racism, Citizen Commission of Human Rights, 2018

8. Williams, Chancellor, The Destruction of Black Civilization, 1987

9. Edward, Jefferson D., Chosen Not Cursed, 1989

10. McKissic, Dwight W., Beyond Roots: In Search of Blacks in the Bible, 1990

Call or Text:
770-240-0089 Press Extension 1
Web: KLEpub.com
Email Services@klepub.com

It's time to start and finish   YOUR Story!

KLE Publishing specializes in helping people become authors. In as little as 15 to 90 days, we can help you develop your books and e-books and publish to 39,000 outlets! We also offer audiobook services.

Write, Edit, Format, Publish
We can help from
Start to Finish.

Explore and learn more about published authors affiliated with KLE.

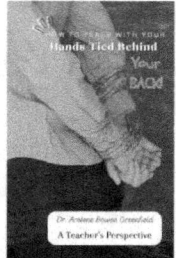    

KLEPub.com

www.ingramcontent.com/pod-product-compliance
Lightning Source LLC
Chambersburg PA
CBHW050044080526
44586CB00014B/1450